CW01044386

Foundations – Faith Life Essentials
Through Repentance to Faith

© 2009 Derek Prince Ministries–International
This publication DPM UK 2019

ISBN 978-1-78263-539-0
Product code: B102D

Scripture quotations are from the New King James Version of the Bible,
Thomas Nelson Publishers, Nashville, TN, © 1982.

This message is a transcript book with questions and study suggestions
added by the Derek Prince Ministries editorial team.

Derek Prince Ministries
www.derekprince.com

EXPANDED
VERSION:
**GROUP
STUDY**

Through
Repentance
to Faith

DPM

DEREK PRINCE MINISTRIES

Contents

About This Study Series... 7

Through Repentance to Faith – an Introduction.................................. 11

Part 1 - The Foundation... 15

Part 2 - The Message of Paul... 41

Part 3 - Faith and Hope 55

About the Author... 69

About This Study Series

The Bible is God's Word and our "instruction manual" to find the path to salvation in Jesus. It then shows us how to walk with Him once we have come to know Him. Logically, therefore, it is a hugely important part of our challenge as Christian believers to study the Word of God.

A sad fact is that very often we forget most of what we have heard quite quickly! As a result, what we have heard often has little impact on the way that we continue to live.

That is why we developed these Study Guides. As Derek Prince has said numerous times in his teaching, "It is a general principle of educational psychology that children remember approximately 40 percent of what they hear; 60 percent of what they hear and see and 80 percent of what they hear, see and do."

This Study Guide is intended to help you to assimilate the truths that you have heard into both your head and into your heart so that they become more than just knowledge and will begin to change the way that you live.

Living the Christian life

This study is part of a series of 10 messages, based on the doctrinal foundation of the Christian life described in Hebrews 6:1-2 which says,

Therefore, leaving the discussion of the elementary principles of Christ, let us go on to perfection, not laying again the foundation of repentance from dead works and of faith

toward God, of the doctrine of baptisms, of laying on of hands, of resurrection of the dead, and of eternal judgment.

This mentions six specific foundation stones that we need to lay before we can build a dwelling place for the Lord in our hearts and lives:

1. Repentance from dead works
2. Faith towards God
3. The doctrine of baptisms – John's baptism, Christian baptism and baptism in the Holy Spirit
4. Laying on of hands
5. Resurrection of the dead
6. Eternal judgment.

When this teaching is applied in your life, with faith, we believe that it will deepen your relationship with God and enable you to live a truly successful Christian life.

How to Study

Each book contains a QR-code (or DVD) that links you to a talk by Derek Prince, the transcript of the talk and questions for personal application or to be discussed in a group setting.

Each video is about an hour long, divided in three parts. Set aside a reasonable length of time to read the Introduction, then watch or read Derek's teaching, and finally come back to the Study Guide to reflect on the Study Questions or to discuss them with your study group.

Once you have completed this series you will find that you have an excellent summary of the teaching. This will help you to share the content with others, whether to a friend, home group or congregation. The more you share the truths you are learning, the more they will become part of your own life and testimony.

Group Study

This study guide has been developed for use by small groups as well as by individuals.

Simply proceed through the material as a team, reflect on the questions and explore the statements together for a rich and rewarding experience.

Scripture to Memorize

In this book, we have chosen key Scriptures for memorization. They will relate in some way to your overall study. Memorizing them will place a spiritual sword in your hands which you, by the Holy Spirit, will be able to use in times of spiritual conflict.

The Word of God has supernatural power for those who will take the time and effort to "hide it in their hearts" by memorizing and meditating on it. As God's Word is hidden in your heart, it becomes constantly available to you for reference, comfort, correction and meditation. Put simply, it becomes part of your life.

Look up the verse in your own Bible and write it in the space provided. You will want to write and say this verse out loud several times until you are confident you know it well. Take time to meditate on the words and their application to your life. As a group, you could talk briefly about the meaning of the verse and its relevance to the lesson or share how you applied it.

You will be asked to recall your Memory Work at the end of the book.

Through Repentance to Faith
– an Introduction

Repentance and faith are two major topics in the Bible. But what do they really mean? How are they related and how can they become part of our lives?

This study will help you discover the importance and the power of both repentance and faith.

The first theme of this study, repentance from dead works, refers to turning away from all things that are not done in faith or obedience.

You will find out what God says about the importance of repentance, a definite decision of the will, and how it is contrasted with remorse. Learn too about the relationship between faith and repentance and how repentance must always precede true faith.

Derek reveals that many of the problems that Christians face are as a result of the fact that they have never truly repented.

As you study this vital topic, ask God to grant you understanding and the desire and ability to truly repent that you might be able to prepare for the next vital step – faith toward God.

Watch the Derek Prince video teaching *Through Repentance to Faith* on YouTube.
Scan the QR-code or visit dpmuk.org/foundations

This video has been divided into three sections, following the chapters in this book. You will find the links to these sections when you tap the 'down arrow' to expand the information about the video.

Write down these verses and try to memorize them.

Hebrews 11:6

No one can please God without
faith, for who ever comes to God must
have faith that God exists and
rewards those who seek him.

Romans 10:9

If you confess that Jesus is
Lord and believe that God
raised him from death, you will
be saved.

MEDITATION

There is no other
way to faith except
through repentance.

The Foundation

In beginning to lay a foundation to a Christian life, most people recognize that it would require faith on our part. But how do we obtain faith? What provisions are there in the Word of God for laying this basic foundation stone?

First, we must see that there is no other way to faith except through repentance. Any other way that claims to get you there is a deception. True faith is impossible without repentance.

In this study series, we have been looking at the central truths of the gospel as presented in Hebrews 6:1–2. This is the third segment of that teaching. To begin this segment, let's go back and briefly recap what we have been studying up to this point.

First of all, the personal foundation of the Christian faith is Jesus Christ. Everyone who is to be a true Christian must build his or her life on that foundation. We see this in the exchange between Jesus and Peter in Matthew 16, when Jesus asked, "Who do you say that I am?" In answer to Jesus' challenging question, Peter declared, "You are the Christ [the Messiah], the Son of the living God" (verse 16). This exchange is a pattern of what needs to happen in each one of our lives in its own particular way. There are four elements to that encounter.

First, confrontation. Jesus and Peter stood face to face. There was no mediator, no priest, no third person in between them.

Second, there was a revelation given by the Spirit of God of the eternal identity of Jesus—not as the carpenter's son, but the Son of the living God.

Third, Peter received and acknowledged that revelation. He did not refuse it, but he embraced it.

Fourth, he made a public confession of his faith. Those four elements must be the basis of every truly successful Christian life: confrontation, revelation, acknowledgment and confession.

Building on the Foundation

Next, we examined a very important practical question. Once we have laid this foundation, how do we build on it? From the parable Jesus told of the wise and the foolish man, we saw that building on this foundation, first of all, consists in acknowledging the Bible as the written Word of God, recognizing Jesus as the living Word, and then hearing and doing what Jesus said. Building on the foundation must involve hearing and doing what Jesus said.

Then we looked at the authority and the power of God's Word. I pointed out that the word authority comes from the word author. The authority of any book depends on the author. The authority of the Bible depends on the Author, who is the Holy Spirit or the Spirit of God—God Himself. The authority of God is in the Bible.

I pointed out that we have the Word in two forms: the written word (the Bible) and the personal word (Jesus, the Word of God made flesh). How we respond to the Word in each form reflects our personal relationship to the Bible. We do not love God any more than we love His Word. We do not obey God any more than we obey His Word. If we want to find out what place God has in our life, we must find out what place the Bible has, because they are the same. The Bible is the written Word; Jesus is the personal Word. Through the written Word the personal Word comes into our lives.

The Doctrinal Foundation

We have looked at the personal foundation, which is Jesus Christ. But the New Testament also reveals that there is a doctrinal foundation. This revelation has escaped the notice of millions of Christians, but it is very clearly stated in Hebrews, which says:

> *Therefore, leaving the discussion of the elementary principles* [basic truths] *of Christ, let us go on to perfection* [completion or maturity], *not laying again the foundation of repentance from dead works and of faith toward God, of the doctrine of baptisms, of laying on of hands, of resurrection of the dead, and of eternal judgment. And this we will do if God permits.*
> *Hebrews 6:1–3*

There are two thoughts portrayed here which we have to combine. First of all, it is essential that we lay the foundation. If we have never laid the foundation, we can never erect the building. Once we have laid the foundation, then we do not keep re-laying the foundation; we go on to complete the building. Those are the two combined thoughts. Hebrews 6:1 speaks of "the foundation." This is the doctrinal foundation of the Christian faith, and it lists six doctrines:

1. Repentance from dead works.
2. Faith toward God.
3. The doctrine of baptisms (plural).
4. The laying on of hands.
5. Resurrection of the dead.
6. Eternal judgment.

If we follow the progression of that list, we will see that it takes us from the very starting point of the Christian faith to its ultimate fulfillment in eternity. It is important for us to see that the Christian faith does not terminate in time—in this life or this world. It takes us beyond this world—beyond time into eternity.

Many Christians today hardly have any vision of eternity. They act and think as if everything that matters is going to happen in time. Actually, Paul says, if only in this life we have faith in Christ, we are of all men the most miserable, the most to be pitied. (See 1 Corinthians 15:19.) If we do not have a vision that takes us beyond time and into eternity, our condition is pitiable and we will suffer many disappointments. Time is not the fulfillment of the Christian life. The fulfillment comes in eternity.

These six doctrines, then, take us from the starting point, which is repentance, right through to the resurrection and the judgment.

If God Permits

Before we begin with the first foundation doctrine, repentance from dead works, I want to first point out a remarkable statement made by the writer of Hebrews in Hebrews 6:3:

This we will do if God permits.

We will go on to completion and fulfillment if God permits. We might ask, "Why would God not permit? Surely He wants us all to go on."

We can answer any question this statement might raise by a simple little example. In any major city of the civilized world today, in order to construct a building you have to have a plan. You have to get a permit from the authorities, and they must approve your plan. Then they come to inspect the building stage by stage as construction continues. But the first aspect of construction they really inspect is the foundation. If the foundation is not to specifications, the building will not be secure. If the foundation is not solid, they will not issue a permit to continue the building.

God deals with you and me in exactly the same way. He says, "I need to inspect your foundation. If it is not laid according to My requirements, I will not give you a permit to go on."

It can be possible to go on forever in this elementary stage of the Christian faith and never mature, never come to completion or fulfillment, because the right foundation was not laid. It is absolutely essential that we master these six doctrines which are the foundation of the Christian faith.

Dead Works

We begin with repentance from dead works. What are dead works? Most of the modern translations say these are works or deeds that lead to death. However, I don't believe that is correct. I think dead works are anything we do that is not done in faith toward God. Anything not done in faith is a dead work. That which brings life into our activity is faith.

You may have been a very good churchgoer. You may have given money to the poor. You may have said prayers. But if it was not done in faith, it was all dead works. We must turn away from everything not done in faith. Faith alone gives life to what we believe and what we do.

That does not necessarily mean that you have been living a sinful life. But it can mean you have just not been alive to God because faith has not come into your heart and brought the life of God into what you do.

Repentance

We need to understand that repentance is not an emotion. Many times preachers will seek to work people up into an emotional attitude and then call them to faith in Christ. But very often that leads to a let-down, because the emotion runs out and they are left with little of any substance.

Bear in mind that repentance, as defined in the Bible, is not an emotion. It is a decision. It does not spring from the emotions. It springs from the will.

If we can reach people's wills and turn their wills, we will see permanent conversions. Many of the so-called "conversions" in the church today are impermanent because they have never really changed the will of the person. In these cases, the people may have had an emotional experience, gotten excited, or maybe even felt wonderful for a few weeks, months or possibly years. But in the end they do not have what it takes to continue on in the Christian life because their wills have not been touched.

As we look further at this subject of repentance, it will help us to understand the meaning of the word.

There are two main languages of the Bible: Greek in the New Testament and Hebrew in the Old. Each of these languages has a specific word for repent. But it is only as we put the two languages together that we get the full meaning of repentance.

The Greek word in secular language is always translated "to change your mind"—change the way you think. So, first of all, repentance is changing your mind about the way you have been living. This might include someone saying, "I have been living to please myself and do my own thing. From now on I am going to live to please Jesus, my Savior." As I said previously, such a recognition is a decision, not an emotion. You can repent without any obvious emotion, but you cannot repent without a change of your will.

The Hebrew word for repentance involves a result. This Hebrew definition is so typical of the Jewish people, because they are a very down-to-earth people. They want to know what result an action will produce. The Hebrew word for repent means literally "to turn around." You have been facing one way—the wrong way, with your back to God—so you turn 180 degrees around, face toward God, and say, "God, here I am. Tell me what to do and I'll do it." If we put the Greek and Hebrew definitions together, we have a complete picture of repentance: it is a decision followed by an action.

Faith follows Repentance

The whole message of the Bible is in this order: repent and believe. There are lots of people who might say they are struggling for faith. The truth is not that they are struggling for faith, but that they may have never met the condition of repentance. Repentance is the first of the six foundation doctrines. If that foundation stone is not in place, the building will always be wobbly.

Over the years, I have counseled hundreds of people, hundreds of Christians who have come to me with their personal problems. After a lot of experience, I came to the conclusion that at least fifty percent of the problems of professing Christians are due to the fact that they have never truly repented.

They have never really changed their mind. They have never really made the decision to surrender to the Lordship of Jesus in their lives. They are still making decisions based on this point of view:
"If I do this, what will it do for me?" If someone has truly repented, that is not the way they think. Instead they think, "If I do this, will it glorify Jesus?"

So we have multitudes of people—especially young people, but not limited to young people—who are double-minded. The Bible says a double-minded man is unstable in all his ways. (See James 1:8.) He does not have a solid foundation. He cannot produce a stable building.

(See James 1:8.)

> **?**
>
> **Right now, quietly reflect on what you have just read and ask yourself: "Have I ever really, truly repented? Or am I still double- minded?**

Is it my aim to please Jesus on Monday, but please myself on Tuesday?" If that is the way you are thinking and living, in actual fact, you have the worst of both worlds. If that is your mindset, you would probably be better off just living in the world, living for yourself—because you are a double-minded person, a split personality.

But if that is, in fact, the way you are thinking and living, take steps now to truly repent and live instead to glorify Jesus.

The Nature of Repentance

There is one parable that Jesus told which is the most vivid and perfect illustration of true repentance. It is the parable of the Prodigal Son. (Somebody once said it should be called "The Caring Father.") The story is found in Luke 15. The second son of a wealthy family decided to get all his inheritance from his father on the spot so he could go off to a distant country and live it up. He did all sorts of sinful things. But then, when he had spent his whole inheritance, a famine came and the only job he could get was feeding pigs. (We must remember that he was

Jewish, so for him to feed pigs was just about as low as he could go—without any slight to present-day pig farmers. It just so happens that for the Jewish people, the pig is one step below a rat in their society.)

So here is the wandering son, in rags, feeding the pigs, hungry, wishing he could fill his stomach with the husks that the pigs are eating. Then this is what happens.

> *"But when he came to himself, he said . . ."*
> *Luke 15:17*

That is the point each of us must come to. It is what I call "the moment of truth." You have to see yourself as you really are. You have to see yourself as God sees you.

> *"But when he came to himself, he said, 'How many of my father's hired servants have bread enough and to spare, and I perish with hunger! I will arise and go to my father, and will say to him, "Father, I have sinned against heaven and before you, and I am no longer worthy to be called your son. Make me like one of your hired servants."'*
> *And he arose and went to his father."*
> *verses 17–20*

True Repentance

Do you see the two elements? He made a decision and then he turned around. That is repentance: making a decision and carrying out your decision.

Repentance means going back to the Father whom you have offended, to the God who loves you, and saying, "I've made a mess of my life. I can't run my own life. I need You. Will You take me back?"

It's wonderful to see how completely he repented and how eager his father was to receive him. He planned to say to his father, "Make me as one of your hired servants." But when he started back from where he had strayed, his father was watching for him. That is how God is. When we begin to turn, He is watching for us and waiting for us. I think this is so beautiful.

The father saw him from a long way off and ran to meet him. The father kissed him, and he never let his son say those last words, "Make me as one of your hired servants." Instead he said:

> *"Bring out the best robe and put it on him, and put a ring on his hand and sandals on his feet. And bring the fatted calf here and kill it, and let us eat and be merry."*
> *verses 22–23*

This is the result of true repentance. And it is worth repenting to be welcomed like that by God.

Just think about that picture for a moment. The prodigal son came to himself. He said, "I've made a mess of my life. I've wasted everything my father gave me. But I'm going to make a decision. I'm going to turn around, I'm going to go back to my father and say I'm sorry." He turned and went. Think about that. That is true repentance, repentance in action.

False Repentance

We need to understand that there can also be a false repentance, which we call remorse. Judas experienced that kind of false repentance, as described in Matthew's gospel:

> *Then Judas, His betrayer, seeing that He had been condemned, was remorseful and brought back the thirty pieces of silver to*

the chief priests and elders, saying, "I have sinned by betraying innocent blood." And they said, "What is that to us? You see to it!" Then he threw down the pieces of silver in the temple and departed, and went and hanged himself.
Matthew 27:3–5

Judas had remorse, but he never changed. In fact, I believe he had passed the point where he could change. To me, this is a solemn thought. In this life, people can pass the point where it is possible for them to change.

The most significant moment in any human life is the moment when God begins to deal with you about repenting. If you shrug your shoulders and say, "I'm not interested. Maybe later," there is no guarantee that God will ever give you the opportunity again. The most critical moment in any human life is the moment when God says, "Repent. I'm willing to take you back. I love you. I want you."

What Makes God Angry?

Considering what I have seen in people's lives and in the Bible, I have come to the conclusion that one action that makes God really angry is despising His grace. He freely offers us His grace, but if we despise it He turns in anger.

One person who despised the grace of God was Esau, and his action is described in Hebrews 12. Let's look at that passage, because there is a lot of Esau in people like you and me. We want to be careful that the Esau in us does not make our decisions.

Pursue peace with all people, and holiness, without which no one will see the Lord: looking carefully [diligently] *lest anyone fall short of the grace of God; lest any root of bitterness springing up cause trouble, and by this many become defiled; lest there*

be any fornicator or profane [godless] person like Esau, who for
one morsel of food sold his birthright.
Hebrews 12:14–16

We have no record whatever that Esau ever committed fornication. But in God's eyes, his attitude was just as bad as fornication. What was his attitude? For one little bowl of soup he despised his birthright. He had the birthright as the elder son—all the inheritance could have gone to him. But just because he was physically hungry and could smell that delicious soup that Jacob had prepared, he gave it up.

This is very vivid to me, because I lived among the Arabs for some time. They make the exact same lentil soup that Jacob made. It has the most delicious smell that permeates the whole house. I can just picture Esau, coming back from his hunting—tired and hungry—and he smells this delicious soup. And Jacob, bargainer that he was, says, "Listen, you sell me your birthright and I'll give you the pottage, the soup."

I suppose Esau thought, *What good will my birthright do me now? I'm hungry. I'll just take what was offered to me.*

The Bible says Esau despised his birthright and he made God extremely angry. Later on, through the prophet Malachi, God said, "Jacob I have loved, Esau I have hated" (Malachi 1:2–3). That is a very solemn thought: If you deliberately despise the grace of God and the inheritance He offers you in Jesus Christ and turn away to pursue some cheap, temporary pleasure of this world, you make God very angry.

Avoiding the Point of No Return

Going on with the message about Esau from Hebrews:

For you know that afterward, when he wanted to inherit the
blessing, he was rejected [by God], for he found no place of

repentance, though he sought it diligently with tears.
Hebrews 12:17

The Greek makes it clear that he was not seeking the place of repentance, but he was seeking the blessing. He was rejected because he found no place—no way—to repent. I believe that in this life, a person can pass the place of repentance and never be able to get back. I want to urge you to consider this, for it is a very solemn thought.

Far too little is said today in congregations and many denominations about the need for repentance. But without true repentance there can never be true faith. You will always have a wobbly, up and down experience—in one day and out the next— because you have not laid the first foundation stone—repentance. Repentance involves a decision of the will to turn away from self- pleasing and doing your own thing to turn back to God. Face up to God and say, "Here I am. Tell me what to do and I'll do it."

Some of you reading this have never truly repented. I want to suggest to you it may well be the source of many of your problems. You feel good one day, have a wonderful meeting in the church, and you think everything is wonderful. The next morning something bad happens and down you go. The problem is that you have never really laid the first foundation stone. All you have is a wobbly edifice that one day will collapse.

Repentance, Then Faith

I want to emphasize that repentance must come before faith. There can be no true faith without repentance. This is emphasized all through the New Testament.

In Matthew chapter 3 we read about the ministry of John the Baptist who was sent to prepare the way for the coming of Jesus the

Messiah. In one word, his message was: "Repent." John the Baptist taught that repentance was essential before the Messiah could come. Repentance prepared the way for the coming of Messiah. Until God's people, Israel, had been through the experience of repentance, they could not be ready to meet their Messiah.

> In those days John the Baptist came preaching in the wilderness of Judea, and saying, "Repent, for the kingdom of heaven is at hand!" For this is he who was spoken of by the prophet Isaiah, saying, "The voice of one crying in the wilderness: 'Prepare the way of the Lord; make His paths straight.'"
> Matthew 3:1–3

How did John the Baptist prepare the way of the Lord? By calling God's people back to repentance. Repentance is the only way we can prepare for the Lord to come into our hearts and lives.

Jesus Continues the Message

Later, when John had finished his course and in fulfillment of His own prophetic word, Jesus Himself came to continue the ministry of the gospel. It says in the gospel of Mark:

> Now after John was put in prison, Jesus came to Galilee, preaching the gospel of the kingdom of God and saying, "The time is fulfilled, and the kingdom of God is at hand. Repent, and believe the gospel."
> Mark 1:14–15

Repent and believe. You cannot truly believe unless you have first repented. The first word of command that ever came from the lips of Jesus was not believe but repent.

I remember being in a meeting in Southeast Asia where a certain preacher had preached a message on healing. He had spoken very eloquently about God's will and His plan to heal. He had quoted many of the promises about healing. But he had not said one word about repentance before he called the people forward.

Most of those who responded to the invitation came from a background of idolatry and they had no idea what they had to do to receive what God was offering. I know, because Ruth and I were both involved in counseling those who came forward. It was such a lesson to me. With all his good intentions and his sweet language, the preacher had totally confused those people, because he gave them the impression that they could come to God without repenting. He never used the word repent once in his message.

I say this not to criticize a preacher, but because I learned a lesson. I believe there are many people in many "gospel" churches who are confused because they are only being told what God will do for them without being told what God requires from them. The first thing He requires is for us to repent—change our mind, turn around, make a 180-degree turn. We must face God and say, "Tell me what to do, and I will do it." That is repentance.

If we look on to the end of Jesus' ministry, His message never changed. After His resurrection, Jesus gave instructions to His disciples. (Remember, this was just before Jesus left this world.)

> Then He said to them, "Thus it is written, and thus it was necessary for the Christ [Messiah] to suffer and to rise from the dead the third day, and that repentance and remission of sins should be preached in His name to all nations, beginning at Jerusalem."
> Luke 24:46–47

Notice the order of the message: repentance first and then remission (or forgiveness) of sins. There is no forgiveness without repentance—and that is the message that was to begin in Jerusalem and be preached to all nations. Repentance, then forgiveness, through His name.

Peter Reiterates the Message

When the Church came into being in public view on the Day of Pentecost, at the great outpouring of the Holy Spirit, a multitude of Jews had gathered and wanted to know what was going on. Peter stood up and preached his famous message from Acts chapter 2. At the end of the message, they were convicted and asked Peter what they had to do. This is the first time the Church, as such, had been asked by sinners what they must do.

> *Now when they heard this* [Peter's message], *they were cut to the heart, and said to Peter and the rest of the apostles,*
> *"Men and brethren, what shall we do?*
> *Acts 2:37*

If you ever come to the place where you sincerely want to know what God wants you to do and you are willing to do it, God will not leave you in any doubt as to what He wants. His difficulty is not in telling you; His difficulty is in bringing you to the place where you want to know and do it.

As soon as these people, under a real conviction of sin, said to the apostles, "Men and brethren, what shall we do?" Peter, as the spokesman of God and the Church, gave them a clear, precise, practical answer:

> *The Peter said to them, "Repent, and let every one of you be baptized in the name of Jesus Christ for the remission* [forgiveness] *of sins; and you shall receive the gift of the Holy Spirit."*
> *verse 38*

The Three-Stage Process

In Peter's response we find a three-stage process.

Number one, repent.

Number two, be baptized in water.

And number three, receive the Holy Spirit.

God's program has never changed. It is exactly what God wants sinners to do today. I believe it is the exact same message the Church should be proclaiming. Repent, be baptized in water and receive the gift of the Holy Spirit.

In places where that message is preached, it happens exactly as it did on the Day of Pentecost. People repent, they are baptized and they receive the Holy Spirit. I have seen this happen many times, where believers, coming up out of the water at baptism, are filled with the Holy Spirit.

Why should we water down the message? We have no authority to do that. The only authority we have is to proclaim the message of the New Testament: repent, be baptized in water, receive the Holy Spirit. When we give the message, God gives the answer. It is not God who has changed, nor the message that has changed. But in many cases it is the Church that has changed.

Let me interject something that may shock you. I cannot find, from the book of Acts onwards, any person who claimed salvation from Jesus without being baptized in water. Check and see if you can find one. Jesus said, "He who believes and is baptized will be saved" (Mark 16:16, emphasis added). What right do we have to take out the words "and is baptized"?

Salvation is believing and being baptized. When you have done that, you are a candidate to receive the Holy Spirit. That is the message of the Church. And it has never changed as far as God is concerned.

Study Questions

1. What special insights did you gain from this lesson?

   To be saved you must believe and be baptised
   To believe you must have faith and
   to receive faith you must repent.

2. Three elements are vital in order to build a strong foundation for your faith:

   - To acknowledge the Bible as the written Word of God
   - To recognize Jesus as the living Word of God
   - Hearing and doing what Jesus said.

   What would change if you left out any of these three elements?

   The foundation would be weak and
   Jesus would not build upon it.
   Your weakness will let you down.
   You will not be saved.

3. Give your own definition of repentance. Consider also using the meaning of the Greek and Hebrew words for repentance to explain the essence of repentance.

It is a decision to turn away from the life we are leading, acknowledge we cannot do it alone, saying sorry for trying and calling upon God to help us and accept us.

4. Do you consider repentance to be something positive or negative? Why?

Positive decision to turn your life around and become what you are meant to be, a son or daughter of the living God, loved & cared for by Him.

5. To many people, the call to repent has a negative meaning. If you were to explain to a non-Christian or a new believer what repentance means, what would you say? (You might want to include elements from the story of the Prodigal Son in Luke 15:11-21 in your answer.)

----

6. Repentance is a change in the way we think and act. Were there specific things in your life that required you to change how you thought and behaved in order to repent and get right with God? Describe the experience.

----

7. Read 1 Corinthians 15:19. Derek Prince states that some Christians act and think as if everything that matters is going to happen in this life. Can you think of any examples from your own life?

----

8. Read Hebrews 12:14-17 and Matthew 27:3-5. What is the difference between true and false repentance? How would you be able to tell the difference?

----

9. Anything that is not done in faith toward God is dead works. But how can prayers or going to church be dead works?

----

10. Read John 3:17-21 and Hebrews 12:14-16. Humanity has a long history of despising God's grace. Ask the Holy Spirit to reveal to you if there are any areas in your life where you don't take God's grace and His gracious gifts seriously enough.

Take time to thank God for what you have learned during this section.

Ask Him to help you apply the teaching so your faith will grow, and so He will be manifested in your life, for His glory.

SUMMARY

- True faith is impossible without repentance.

- We must turn away from everything not done in faith. Faith alone gives life to what we believe and what we do.

- Repentance, as defined in the Bible, is not an emotion. It is a decision followed by an action. The Greek word for repentance means "to change your mind". The Hebrew word means "to turn around."

- God's will for all people is for them to repent, to be baptized in water and to be filled with the Holy Spirit.

What is righteousness? It is like asking to know what crooked is. I would simply show you a straight line. Anything that deviates from that straight line is crooked. In the same way, anything that is not righteous is sinful.

The Message of Paul

Let's look at the ministry of Paul, the great apostle to the Gentiles, as it is recorded in the book of Acts. First of all, Paul found himself in Athens, which was a very intellectual and idolatrous city. He ended up by preaching to them. Really, I don't think he had any intention of preaching to them. However, the people wanted to know what he believed and he ended up telling them, as he concluded his message in verses 30 and following of Acts 17. Speaking about all the time that humanity had lived in idolatry and ignorance of God, Paul said:

> *"Truly, these times of ignorance God overlooked, but now commands all men everywhere to repent . . ."*
> *Acts 17:30*

That verse says it so clearly: God now commands all men everywhere to repent. No place and no person is omitted. It is God's universal requirement from humanity. He is willing to overlook the past if we will repent.

Jesus as Judge

And then, Paul continues:

". . . because He [God] has appointed a day on which He will judge the world in righteousness by the Man whom He has ordained. He has given assurance of this to all by raising Him from the dead. Verse 31

Here we notice another feature of the preaching of the apostles which is often omitted: Jesus is not only the Savior, He is also the Judge. Jesus is just as thorough and efficient in judgment as He is in salvation. If we do not meet Him as Savior, we will meet Him as Judge.

This truth has been left out of so much preaching. People talk about the Savior but they never mention the Judge. Actually, in his message to the men of Athens, Paul never mentioned a Savior—all he mentioned was the Judge.

People will live very different lives if they are not aware of the fact that they will one day face the judgment of Jesus. There is a carelessness and sloppiness in much of contemporary Christianity because we have not faced up to the fact that not only is Jesus the Savior—He is also the Judge. "God has appointed a day on which He will judge the world in righteousness."

The Key Issue—Righteousness

The issue of judgment is righteousness—how we have lived, what kind of people we have been. It is not a question of our denomination, nationality, or social status. There is only one issue in judgment— righteousness.

In his first epistle, John said, "All unrighteousness is sin" (1 John 5:17). People may ask for a definition of what righteousness is. In many ways, it is like asking to know what crooked is. I am not a geometrician, but to answer that question, I would simply show you a straight line. Anything that deviates from that straight line is crooked.

It may deviate by one degree or it may deviate by ninety degrees, but it is still crooked. In the same way, all unrighteousness is sin. Anything that is not righteous is sinful. There is no third category.

Many believers today have a third category: It is not righteous, but it is not sinful either. That category does not exist in God's thinking—anything that is not righteous is sinful.

Not Holding Back

Let's look on to Acts 20, which is Paul's description of his ministry in Ephesus where he had some of the greatest results of his whole ministry. He is speaking in Acts 20 to the elders of the church in Ephesus because he was about to leave them. He says, "You will see my face no more [in this world]" (Acts 20:25). And he has a message of love and concern for those men. About his ministry in Ephesus, he says:

> *"I kept back nothing that was helpful ..."*
> *Acts 20:20*

I have often pondered on that phrase: "I kept back nothing." It implies that a person might be motivated not to preach the full truth because it might cost you your social position. Or, if you are a minister in a certain denomination, it might cost you your position in the denomination. If you are a society figure, it might cost you your popularity. But Paul says, "I thought it over and I decided that nothing was going to influence me to keep back any of the message."

> *"I kept back nothing that was helpful [or profitable], but proclaimed it to you, and taught you publicly and from house to house . . ." Verse 20*

I like the fact that Paul's message did not change whether it was in a big meeting or in a home group. It was the same message. What was the message?

> "... testifying to Jews, and also to Greeks, repentance toward God and faith toward our Lord Jesus Christ."
> verse 21

What comes first, faith or repentance? Repentance toward God. First you say, "God, I'm sorry. I've been a sinner. I've led my own life." Then comes faith toward Jesus. That's where you say, "Jesus, I believe You took my place. You died for me on the cross. You took my sins." But you cannot have true faith in Jesus unless you first have true repentance toward God.

The New Testament is so consistent on this point. The Church needs to repent. We have often watered down the message, deceived people, and given them a false impression of what it means to become a real Christian. You cannot become a real Christian without repentance. There is no faith without repentance.

All Men Everywhere

The Bible says "all men everywhere" have to repent. (See Acts 17:30.) You might ask, "Why all men everywhere?" Let me answer you from the prophet Isaiah.

> All we like sheep have gone astray;
> We have turned, every one, to his own way ...
> Isaiah 53:6

That is our problem: we have turned to our own way. We may not have necessarily committed murder or idolatry or stolen anything—or even lied. But we have all done one thing: we have turned to our own way. Our way is not God's way. It is one thing we all have in common, regardless of our denominational, racial, or social background. We have all turned to our own way.

Then Isaiah says:

The Lord has laid on Him [Jesus] *the iniquity of us all. verse 6*

Iniquity is a very strong word. It is turning to our own way. It is outright rebellion—putting myself ahead of God. That is why God requires all men everywhere to repent. Because we have all turned to our own way. We have all been doing our own thing, pleasing ourselves and leaving God out of the picture. God says, "I will accept you. I will forgive you because of what Jesus did—if you will repent." The bottom line is repentance.

Repentance Begins with God

Everything good starts with God. We must recognize that we are always dependent on the grace of God. Apart from God's grace, apart from the moving of His Spirit, we cannot repent. This is brought out so clearly in Psalm 80, where the same phrase occurs three times:

Restore us, O God, Cause Your face to shine,
And we shall be saved! Verse 3
Restore us, O God of hosts; Cause Your face to shine,
And we shall be saved! Verse 7
Restore us, O Lord God of hosts; Cause Your face to shine,
And we shall be saved! Verse 19

Where this modern translation says, "restore us," the Hebrew says, "turn us back"—in other words, "cause us to repent." It is reiterated three times: in verses 3, 7, and 19:

Turn us back, O God . . . and we shall be saved.
Turn us back . . . and we shall be saved.
Turn us back, O Lord . . . and we shall be saved.

You cannot repent unless God turns you. The turning starts with God. That is why it is such a vital moment in our lives when God begins to turn us. Because if we shrug it off and turn away, we cannot repent left to ourselves. We are dependent on God to initiate repentance.

"Turn Us Back" Again

The book of Lamentations is the mourning of Jeremiah over the destruction of Jerusalem because of its continued rebellion against God. In Lamentations 5:21, in this translation, the words "turn us back" are used—but it is the same word that is used in Psalm 80:

Turn us back to you, O Lord, and we will be restored [or returned].
Lamentations 5:21

What Jeremiah is praying, in other words, is: "Lord, please turn us back and we will turn." This is a very solemn thought. You cannot turn unless God starts to turn you. That is why it is such a sensitive moment in every life when God initiates the process of repentance.

I know of one young man who was my companion in the army. When I got saved he was the only witness, and he knew very well of the change in my life. Later on in the same unit, I started a Bible class. I thought, I've got to do something. I had no idea how to run a Bible class, not even where to begin. So I thought, begin at the New Testament, in chapter 1. So I began with the genealogy of Jesus.

I had about four or five of my fellow soldiers attending this class in the desert in North Africa. Then this good friend of mine came to me and said, "I'm sorry, old chap, but I won't be coming to your Bible study anymore." I said, "Why not?" He said, "Because I know if I do I will be converted."

Years later I met him in a totally different circumstance. He was the most miserable person I ever had met! And by then he had changed his tune. He pleaded with me to help him and I did everything I could. In all humility, I can say that I have had a great deal of experience in leading people to the Lord. But frighteningly, I could not help him. I had helped his wife, and she was saved. But not him. In subsequent years, I lost contact with him, so I do not know what his end was. But, oh, what a warning his experience was to me! He wanted me to help him convert to Christ and I could not and he did not.

You may think you can turn whenever you want to turn. You think you can say, "God, I'm busy now, but come back later." You cannot do that. When my friend wanted to turn, he could not.

Repent or Perish

The Bible says there is only one alternative to repentance, and that is to perish. We see this stated in the first few verses in Luke 13, in the ministry of Jesus:

> There were present at that season some who told Him about the Galileans whose blood Pilate had mingled with their sacrifices. Luke 13:1

Apparently Pilate had them executed while they were actually performing some sacrifice. You would think that would count for their good, but Jesus answered and said:

> "Do you suppose that these Galileans were worse sinners than all other Galileans, because they suffered such things? I tell you , no; but unless you repent you will all likewise perish. Or those eighteen on whom the tower in Siloam fell and killed them, do you think that they were worse sinners than all other men who dwelt in Jerusalem? I tell you, no; but unless you repent you will all likewise perish." verses 2–5

Study Questions

1. What special insights did you gain from this lesson?

    ----

2. Throughout the New Testament, repentance stands out as the first essential requirement from God. Compare Mark 1:4-5, 14-15, Acts 3:19, 17:30 and Acts 20:20-21. Why is repentance of such importance?

    ----

3. Jesus is not only the Savior, He is also the Judge. When will we meet Jesus as Savior? When will we meet Him as Judge?

....

....

....

....

Write down (or discuss) any associations you might have with these words.

Jesus is Savior	Jesus is Judge

Now take time to pray about both aspects of Jesus ministry.

4. Repentance involves a decision of the will to turn away from self-pleasing and doing your own thing, and to turn back to God. Apply this principle to the different areas in your life, such as your marriage, your attitude towards your job, your money, the way you spend your time, the choice of your church, the way you think about the future or how you behave in traffic. Ask the Holy Spirit to reveal to you if there is anything specific that you still need to repent from.

....

....

....

....

5. The process of repentance is initiated by God. See Psalm 80:3,7,19 and Lamentations 5:21. Does this mean we are to remain passive? (See also James 4:8)

    ----

6. The Bible says all men everywhere have to repent. We haven't necessarily committed murder or idolatry, or stolen anything, or maybe not even lied. So, why all men everywhere? Read Isaiah 53:6 and give your answer.

    ----

7. Read Luke 13:3 and 5. In talking about some Galileans, whom Pilate had apparently killed while they were making sacrifices, and another 18 people who were killed when a tower fell on them, Jesus says there is only one alternative to repentance. What is it? How does this make you feel?

....

....

8. Now that you realise the teaching on repentance and faith is so essential to the Christian life, take some time to pray for all ministers, pastors and youth leaders within the Church to preach the same message as Jesus Christ: to repent and believe the Gospel.

....

....

....

....

Take time to thank God for what you have learned during this section.

Ask Him to help you apply the teaching so your faith will grow, and so He will be manifested in your life, for His glory.

SUMMARY

- Jesus is not only the Savior, He is also the Judge. If we do not meet Him as Savior, we will meet Him as Judge.

- Anything that is not righteous is sinful. There is no third category.

- We may not have necessarily committed murder or idolatry or stolen anything—or even lied. But we have all done one thing: we have turned to our own way. Therefore all men everywhere need to repent.

- Apart from God's grace, apart from the moving of His Spirit, we cannot repent. That is why it is such a sensitive moment in every life when God initiates the process of repentance.

- The Bible says there is only one alternative to repentance, and that is to perish.

In the Bible, faith is always

based on the Word of God.

Anything that is not based

on the Word of God

is not biblical faith.

Faith and Hope

We now turn our attention to consider a little bit about the nature of faith, which is the positive outcome of repentance. Romans 10:17 says,

"Faith comes by hearing, and hearing by the word of God."

This is a very important principle. Faith, as used in the Bible, always means faith in the Word of God. Faith can come only from one source: God's Word. It has only one focus: God's Word.

It's fairly common for us to say, in contemporary English, "I have great faith in my doctor," or, "I have faith in a political party," or faith in something else. It is legitimate to talk about placing confidence in that way—there is nothing wrong with that concept. But it is not the scriptural way to use the word faith. In the Bible faith is always based on the Word of God. Anything that is not based on the Word of God is not biblical faith.

In Hebrews 11 we find the definition of faith. I think it is the only word that the Bible actually defines; I cannot think of another word that is actually defined in the Bible.

Faith is the substance of things hoped for, the evidence [a sure persuasion] of [concerning] things not seen.
Hebrews 11:1

We see there a relationship between faith and hope. I have discovered that a lot of people have hope when they think they have faith. Faith is here and now; hope is for the future. Faith is a substance— something so real that it is actually called a substance. On the basis of faith, we can have a legitimate hope for the future. But, any hope that is not based on legitimate faith is just wishful thinking.

It is important for us to recognize that faith is in our hearts—in fact, faith is a substance in our hearts. It is right here right now.

> *If you confess with your mouth the Lord Jesus* [or Jesus as Lord] *and believe in your heart . . . you will be saved. For with the heart one believes . . . to salvation.*
> Romans 10:9–10

Notice again in this verse that biblical faith is not in the mind. It is in the heart.

Faith in the Heart

In the New Testament, believing is a word of motion: it is not a static thing. Neither is believing simply taking an intellectual position. It is something in your heart that leads you to something new. Like believing, faith is a word of motion. By faith we believe unto salvation. You can have intellectual faith and never be changed. You can embrace all the doctrines of the Bible intellectually and remain completely the same. But when you have faith in your heart, it leads to salvation.

Faith is in the present; hope is in the future. Faith is in the heart; hope is in the mind.

In 1 Thessalonians Paul speaks about both. It is a very interesting picture that he uses.

*But let us who are of the day be sober, putting on the breast-
plate of faith and love, and as a helmet the hope of salvation.*
1 Thessalonians 5:8

You will notice two items of armor in this passage: the breastplate and the helmet. Faith is the breastplate, and it protects the heart. Hope is the helmet, and it protects the head. Faith is in the heart; hope is in the mind.

Hope is very important, because every true Christian should be an optimist. If someone is a pessimist, actually it is a denial of their faith.

I define hope this way: a confident expectation of good based on the Word of God. Every one of us who is a true believer has a confident expectation of good. No matter what happens in this life, we are going to be with Jesus forever. If that is your hope, you may temporarily get depressed or feel downcast. But you never give up because you have a hope—a hope that is based on faith.

Four Faith Statements

Let us look again at Hebrews 11 for some more statements about faith. (This wonderful eleventh chapter of Hebrews is known as the great "faith chapter.")

1. Faith Relates to the Unseen

By faith we understand that the world [or ages] *were framed*
by the word of God, so that the things which are seen were not
made of things which are visible.
Hebrews 11:3

It is so important to understand that faith relates us to the invisible. Faith is not based on what we see. Faith takes us beyond the realm of the senses into the realm of the invisible.

In 2 Corinthians 5:7, Paul says, "We walk by faith, not by sight." Notice that these are alternatives. When we see, we do not need to believe. We only need to believe when we do not see. Paul says, "We walk by faith." We are not walking by what we see. We are walking by what we believe.

Outside the tomb of Lazarus, Jesus said to Martha:

"Did I not say to you that if you would believe you would see the glory of God?"
John 11:40

According to Jesus, which comes first—believing or seeing? People often say, "When I see it, I'll believe it." But that is not true, because when you see, you do not need to believe. You need to believe when you cannot see. "We walk by faith, not by sight."

I have met so many people who say, "If I only could see, I'd believe." But that is not true, for then you would not need to believe. You need to believe when you can't see. "We walk by faith, not by sight."

2.   *Faith Is Primarily Character*

In the original languages of both Greek and Hebrew, faith is not primarily a doctrinal issue. It is a matter of character. We have it all wrong in our evangelical thinking. We tend to talk about faith as an intellectual embracing of certain doctrines. However, faith is primarily a matter of character. This is true of the words for faith in the Hebrew (emunah) and the Greek (pistis). Both primarily mean "faithfulness, loyalty, commitment."

Jesus said to His disciples, "You are those who have continued with Me in My trials" (Luke 22:28). That is faith. It is continuing with Jesus. It is a personal commitment to a Person—Jesus.

3.   *Faith Brings Confession*

Faith relates us to Jesus as our High Priest, as we confess that He is our Lord.

> *Consider the Apostle and High Priest of our confession,*
> *Christ Jesus.*
> *Hebrews 3:1*

Remember that very important fact. Jesus is the High Priest of your confession. If you say it, He is your High Priest. If you keep silent, He cannot be your High Priest. That is why it is so important to confess your faith.

> *Seeing then that we have a great High Priest who has passed*
> *through the heavens, Jesus the Son of God, let us hold fast our*
> *confession.*
> *Hebrews 4:14*

We confess, then we are tested, but we hold fast. And as long as we hold fast, Jesus is our High Priest.

Hebrews 10 takes us one stage further:

> *Having a High Priest over the house of God. . . . Let us hold fast*
> *the confession of our hope without wavering.*
> *Hebrews 10:21, 23*

Notice that now we have progressed from faith to hope. We have a hope based on our faith. We confess our faith and now we confess our hope.

Hebrews 10:23 also says "without wavering." Why do you think it says without wavering? Why would it say that we must hold fast the profession of our faith? The reason is because there will be forces that will oppose us, pressures that will come against us, and circumstances designed to discourage us and undermine our faith. The life of faith is a battle of determination and endurance, and our obligation is to "not waver."

4.   *Faith Will Be Tested*

Finally, I have to tell you, reluctantly, faith will be tested. Untested faith is of no value in the sight of God. Jesus said to the church of Ephesus:

> *"I counsel you to buy from Me gold refined* [tried] *in the fire."*
> *Revelation 3:18*

The faith Jesus describes here is real faith that has stood the test. In ancient times, gold that had not been tested by fire was not considered worth anything. Faith that has not been tested is not valued at all by God.

A Time for Endurance

In closing, let me quote James 1:2–4:

> *Count it all joy when you fall into various trials, knowing that*
> *the testing of your faith produces patience* [endurance].
> *But let patience* [endurance] *have its perfect work,*
> *that you may be perfect and complete, lacking nothing.*

Do you want to be perfect and complete? You must let endurance have its "perfect work." That is the trial that you must go through. Peter says elsewhere:

> *In this greatly rejoice, though now for a little while, if need be,*
> *you have been grieved by various trials, that the genuineness*

of your faith, being much more precious than gold that
perishes, though it is tested by fire, may be found to praise,
honor and glory at the revelation [appearing] *of Jesus Christ.*
1 Peter 1:6–7

Let me simply say one final word to you, which you may wish I had not said: there is only one way to learn endurance in your walk of faith. And that is by enduring. But if we endure, and when we come through the testing of our faith successfully, we will fulfill what we have been created for. Our lives will bring praise, honor and glory to our Lord Jesus Christ.

PRAYER

Father, I desire that faith be built up in me.
I repent of my sins. I turn away from them
and turn toward You. I confess now that I
have grieved You in some ways (name them).
I put my trust in You to cleanse me and to
finish the work You have begun in me. Help
me to persevere through trials, so that when
I am tested I might be found perfect and
complete, lacking nothing.
This I pray in Jesus' name. Amen.

Study Questions

1. What special insights did you gain from this lesson?

   ----

2. Repentance is the only way to biblical faith. But what is faith? Give your own definition. Are there different kinds of faith? What is biblical faith?

   ----

3. Read Romans 10:10, 2 Corinthians 5:7 and 1 Thessalonians 5:8. How do faith and hope relate? What is the difference?

---

4. How can pessimism be a denial of your faith?

---

5. Reflect on Romans 10:13-17. These verses are often quoted in sermons and Bible studies and might therefore, have lost their meaning to you. Ask the Holy Spirit to speak to you through these verses. Write down or discuss anything that stands out for you and pray about it.

---

6. Read 2 Corinthians 5:7 and John 11:39-40. Followers of Jesus walk by faith, not by sight. Is there a situation where you need to strengthen your faith in God's Word and His faithfulness and to turn away from what your senses are telling you?

----

7. Think of two situations or areas in your life where you have had to
   exercise faith in a specific promise of God. Answer the following
   questions about each of those areas:

   · What specific promise(s) did you claim?
   · What conflicts came because you chose to trust in God's
     promises? These conflicts could be internal (fear, doubt, etc.)
     or external (problems with friends or family, etc.)
   · What results have you seen because you took a stand on the
     promises of God? (Either in yourself or in the circumstances.)

----

8. Faith is not primarily a doctrinal issue, but a matter of staying faithful
   to Jesus in all situations and circumstances. Is there a situation in
   your life where you are tempted to ignore or distrust Jesus and His
   commands? What is making it difficult for you to trust and obey Him?

----

9. Jesus is the High Priest of your confession. Throughout history, churches have developed several faith confessions, such as the Nicene Creed or the Westminster Confession of Faith. Have a go at writing your own confession. What vital elements do you believe about God, for both today and eternity?

----

10. Faith will be tested. Read 2 Chronicles 32:30-31 and Deuteronomy 8:2-5. These two stories show that God sometimes tests our faith. How does He test us? For what purpose? Share about, or write down, the times your faith was tested. What happened? How did you respond? What was the result?

As you finish this study, ask for God's help to apply the truths from this study to your life. Pray that a new desire to live a life of faith before God will be born in your heart.

SUMMARY

- Faith can come only from one source: God's Word. Anything that is not based on the Word of God is not biblical faith. (Romans 10:17)

- On the basis of faith, we can have a legitimate hope for the future. But, any hope that is not based on legitimate faith is just wishful thinking. (Hebrews 11:1) Faith is in the present; hope is in the future. Faith is in the heart; hope is in the mind.

- Hope is a confident expectation of good based on the Word of God. Every one of us who is a true believer has a confident expectation of good.

- Faith is not based on what we see. Faith takes us beyond the realm of the senses into the realm of the invisible. (2 Corinthians 5:7, Hebrews 11:3)

- Faith is not primarily a doctrinal issue. According to the meaning of the Greek and Hebrew words for faith, it is a matter of faithfulness, loyalty and commitment to Jesus.

- Jesus is the High Priest of your confession. If you say it, He is your High Priest. If you keep silent, He cannot be your High Priest. That is why it is so important to confess your faith.

- Faith will be tested. If we want to be perfect and complete, we must let endurance have its "perfect work." (James 1:2–4)

In the next study, *Faith and Works*, you will deepen your understanding of the difference between law and grace and how to avail yourself of God's grace.

Recall and write down the verses you memorized
at the beginning of this book:

Hebrews 11:6

Romans 10:9

About the Author

Derek Prince (1915–2003) was born in India of British parents. He was educated as a scholar of Greek and Latin at Eton College and King's College, Cambridge in England. Upon graduation he held a fellowship (equivalent to a professorship) in Ancient and Modern Philosophy at King's College. Prince also studied Hebrew, Aramaic, and modern languages at Cambridge and the Hebrew University in Jerusalem. As a student, he was a philosopher and self-proclaimed agnostic.

Bible Teacher

While in the British Medical Corps during World War II, Prince began to study the Bible as a philosophical work. Converted through a powerful encounter with Jesus Christ, he was baptized in the Holy Spirit a few days later. Out of this encounter, he formed two conclusions: first, that Jesus Christ is alive; second, that the Bible is a true, relevant, up-to-date book. These conclusions altered the whole course of his life, which he then devoted to studying and teaching the Bible as the Word of God.

Discharged from the army in Jerusalem in 1945, he married Lydia Christensen, founder of a children's home there. Upon their marriage, he immediately became father to Lydia's eight adopted daughters – six Jewish, one Palestinian Arab, and one English. Together, the family saw the rebirth of the state of Israel in 1948. In the late 1950s, they adopted another daughter while Prince was serving as principal of a teacher training college in Kenya.

In 1963, the Princes immigrated to the United States and pastored a church in Seattle. In 1973, Prince became one of the founders of Intercessors for America. His book Shaping History through Prayer and Fasting has awakened Christians around the world to their responsibility to pray for their governments. Many consider underground translations of the book as instrumental in the fall of communist regimes in the USSR, East Germany, and Czechoslovakia.

Lydia Prince died in 1975, and Prince married Ruth Baker (a single mother to three adopted children) in 1978. He met his second wife, like his first wife, while she was serving the Lord in Jerusalem. Ruth died in December 1998 in Jerusalem, where they had lived since 1981.

Teaching, Preaching and Broadcasting

Until a few years before his own death in 2003 at the age of eighty-eight, Prince persisted in the ministry God had called him to as he traveled the world, imparting God's revealed truth, praying for the sick and afflicted, and sharing his prophetic insights into world events in the light of Scripture. Internationally recognized as a Bible scholar and spiritual patriarch, Derek Prince established a teaching ministry that spanned six continents and more than sixty years.

He is the author of more than fifty books, six hundred audio teachings, and one hundred video teachings, many of which have been translated and published in more than one hundred languages. He pioneered teaching on such groundbreaking themes as generational curses, the biblical significance of Israel, and demonology. Prince's radio program, which began in 1979, has been translated into more than a dozen languages and continues to touch lives. Derek's main gift of explaining the Bible and its teaching in a clear and simple way has helped build a foundation of faith in millions of lives. His nondenominational, nonsectarian approach has made his teaching equally relevant and helpful to people from all racial and religious backgrounds, and his teaching is estimated to have reached more than half the globe.

DPM Worldwide Ministry

In 2002, he said, "It is my desire – and I believe the Lord's desire – that this ministry continue the work, which God began through me over sixty years ago, until Jesus returns." Derek Prince Ministries International continues to reach out to believers in over 140 countries with Derek's teaching, fulfilling the mandate to keep on "until Jesus returns." This is accomplished through the outreaches of more than thirty Derek Prince offices around the world, including primary work in Australia, Canada, China, France, Germany, the Netherlands, New Zealand, Norway, Russia, South Africa, Switzerland, the United Kingdom, and the United States.

For current information about these and other worldwide locations, visit **www.derekprince.com.**

FOUNDATIONS
faith life essentials

www.dpmuk.org/shop

This book is part of a series of 10 studies on the foundations of the Christian faith.

Order the other books to get everything you need to develop a strong, balanced, Spirit-filled life!

1. Founded on the Rock

There is only one foundation strong enough for the Christian life, and we must be sure our lives are built on Jesus Himself.

2. Authority and Power of God's Word

Both the Bible and Jesus Christ are identified as the Word of God. Learn how Jesus endorsed the authority of Scripture and how to use God's Word as a two-edged sword yourself.

3. Through Repentance to Faith

What is faith? And how can you develop it? It starts with repentance: to change the way we think and to begin acting accordingly.

4. Faith and Works

Many Christians live in a kind of twilight - halfway between law and grace. They do not know which is which nor how to avail themselves of God's grace.

5. The Doctrine of Baptisms

A baptism is a transition - out of an old way of living into a totally new way of living. All of our being is involved. This study explains the three different forms of baptism presented in the Bible.

6. Immersion in the Spirit

Immersion can be accomplished in two ways: the swimming pool way and the Niagara Falls way. This book takes a closer look at the Niagara Falls experience, which relates to the baptism of the Holy Spirit.

7. Transmitting God's Power

Laying on of hands is one of the basic tenets of the Christian faith. By it, we may transmit God's blessing and authority and commission someone for service. Discover this Biblical doctrine!

8. At The End of Time

In this study, Derek Prince reveals the nature of eternity and outlines what lies ahead in the realm of end-time events.

9. Resurrection of the Body

The death and resurrection of Jesus produced a change in the universe. Derek explains here how the resurrection of Jesus impacted man's spirit, soul, and body.

10. Final Judgment

This book examines the four major, successive scenes of judgment in eternity. Exploring the distinctive aspects of these four judgments, Derek opens the Scriptures to bring forth treasures hidden there.

Christian Foundations Course

If you have enjoyed this study and would like to deepen your knowledge of God's Word and apply the teaching – why not enrol on Derek Prince's Christian Foundations Bible Course?

Building on the Foundations of God's Word

A detailed study of the six essential doctrines of Christianity found in Hebrews 6:1-2.

- Scripture-based curriculum
- Practical, personal application
- Systematic Scripture memorisation
- Opportunity for questions and personal feedback from course tutor
- Certificate upon completion
- Modular based syllabus
- Set your own pace
- Affordable
- Based on *Foundational Truths for Christian Living*

For a prospectus, application form and pricing information, please visit www.dpmuk.org, call 01462 492100 or send an e-mail to enquiries@dpmuk.org

Foundational Truths For Christian Living

Develop a strong, balanced, Spirit-filled life, by discovering the foundations of faith: salvation; baptism, the Holy Spirit, laying on hands, the believers' resurrection and eternal judgment.

Its reader-friendly format includes a comprehensive index of topics and a complete index of Scripture verses used in the book.

ISBN 978-1-908594-82-2
Paperback and eBook
£ 13.99

www.dpmuk.org/shop

More best-sellers by Derek Prince

- Blessing or Curse: You can Choose
- Bought with Blood
- Life-Changing Spiritual Power
- Marriage Covenant
- Prayers & Proclamations
- Self-Study Bible Course
- Shaping History Through Prayer and Fasting
- Spiritual Warfare for the End Times
- They Shall Expel Demons
- Who is the Holy Spirit?

For more titles: www.dpmuk.org/shop

Inspired by Derek's teaching?

Help make it available to others!

If you have been inspired and blessed by this Derek Prince resource you can help make it available to a spiritually hungry believer in other countries, such as China, the Middle East, India, Africa or Russia.

Even a small gift from you will ensure that that a pastor, Bible college student or a believer elsewhere in the world receives a free copy of a Derek Prince resource in their own language.

**Donate now: www.dpmuk.org/give
or visit www.derekprince.com**

Derek Prince Ministries

DPM–Asia/Pacific
38 Hawdon Street
Sydenham
Christchurch 8023
New Zealand
T: + 64 3 366 4443
E: admin@dpm.co.nz
W: www.dpm.co.nz

DPM–Australia
15 Park Road
Seven Hills
New South Wales 2147
Australia
T: +61 2 9838 7778
E: enquiries@au.derekprince.com
W: www.derekprince.com.au

DPM–Canada
P. O. Box 8354
Halifax
Nova Scotia B3K 5M1
Canada
T: + 1 902 443 9577
E: enquiries.dpm@eastlink.ca
W: www.derekprince.org

DPM–France
B.P. 31, Route d'Oupia
34210 Olonzac
France
T: + 33 468 913872
E: info@derekprince.fr
W: www.derekprince.fr

DPM–Germany
Söldenhofstr. 10
83308 Trostberg
Germany
T: + 49 8621 64146
E: ibl@ibl-dpm.net
W: www.ibl-dpm.net

DPM-Netherlands
Nijverheidsweg 12
7005 BJ, Doetinchem
Netherlands
T: +31 251-255044
E: info@derekprince.nl
W: www.derekprince.nl

Offices Worldwide

DPM–Norway
P. O. Box 129
Lodderfjord
N-5881 Bergen
Norway
T: +47 928 39855
E: sverre@derekprince.no
W: www.derekprince.no

Derek Prince Publications Pte. Ltd.
P. O. Box 2046
Robinson Road Post Office
Singapore 904046
T: + 65 6392 1812
E: dpmchina@singnet.com.sg
W: www.dpmchina.org (English)
     www.ygmweb.org (Chinese)

DPM–South Africa
P. O. Box 33367
Glenstantia
0010 Pretoria
South Africa
T: +27 12 348 9537
E: enquiries@derekprince.co.za
W: www.derekprince.co.za

DPM–Switzerland
Alpenblick 8
CH-8934 Knonau
Switzerland
T: + 41 44 768 25 06
E: dpm-ch@ibl-dpm.net
W: www.ibl-dpm.net

DPM–UK
PO Box 393
Hitchin SG5 9EU
United Kingdom
T: + 44 1462 492100
E: enquiries@dpmuk.org
W: www.dpmuk.org

DPM–USA
P. O. Box 19501
Charlotte NC 28219
USA
T: + 1 704 357 3556
E: ContactUs@derekprince.org
W: www.derekprince.org

Lightning Source UK Ltd.
Milton Keynes UK
UKHW021657130720
366461UK00005B/143